IMRAN LEARNS ABOUT ALLAH

by
Sajda Nazlee

Published by
Ta-Ha Publishers
1, Wynne Road,
London SW9 0BD, United Kingdom

Copyright © 1414/1994, Ta-Ha Publishers Ltd.
First published January 1994

Reprinted : October 1999 / Rajab 1420

Published by:

Ta-Ha Publishers Ltd.
1 Wynne Road
London SW9 0BB

By: Sajda Nazlee
General Editor: Afsar Siddiqui
Edited by: Abdassamad Clarke
Illustrated by: M. Ishaq

British Library Cataloguing in Publication Data
Nazlee, Sajda
Imran Learns About Allah
I. Title

ISBN 1-897940-09-2

Typeset by: BookWright, Isle of Lewis.

Printed by: De-luxe Printers, London NW10 7NR.

Imran Learns About Allah

Imran walked home from school one hot summers afternoon with his cousin and best friend Uthman. It was a wonderful baking hot day. Both boys decided to take the long route home through the outskirts of town. As they walked they came across an enormous house with a wonderful, great big garden. In the garden there were six apple trees loaded with beautiful rosy red apples.

"What an amazing garden! What delicious looking apples!" exclaimed Imran. He stared at the apples. Both boys pressed their faces against the gates of the garden. They peered through at those tempting apples.

"I'm sure they're really juicy," said Uthman. He turned his big green eyes towards his friend. Imran was looking far ahead into the garden to see what else he could spot.

"I think this is a really interesting garden," mused Imran. He almost pushed his friend out of the way. He tried to get a better view from where he was standing.

Both boys agreed that nobody seemed to be watching. They would have a little tour around the garden. They wanted to find out what more they could discover.

"This must belong to a really rich person," said Imran as he ambled in. Uthman followed him, secretly convinced that the garden belonged to a king. As they walked further into the garden, to their huge surprise they came across a swimming pool.

"A swimming pool!" cried Uthman, thrilled to bits.

The water looked so cool and refreshing. The pool had a deep end and a shallow end. Imran and Uthman both loved swimming and were like two fishes in the water.

"Come on Imran! Let's swim in the shallow end," said Uthman, gazing on the water in excitement.

"OK. Nobody is watching us. Let's enjoy ourselves," said Imran, throwing his shirt in the air, "And if still nobody is watching us we'll sit on that seesaw. And we'll eat some of those delicious-looking apples."

Both boys jumped into the water with a great splash. They found that it was wonderfully cool. First they swam a little and then they played at splashing each other. After they had enough of swimming they climbed out of the pool. Then they realised that they had no towels to dry themselves with.

"I've an idea," said Imran, his eyes wide with excitement, "Let's pluck some apples from one of the trees and eat them as we play on the seesaw. Then we can dry out at the same time, before dressing."

So over they went hotfoot to the apple trees. Imran, who was a little taller than Uthman, sat his friend on his shoulders. It was then easy for Uthman to reach the branches of the tree.

Meanwhile, Mr. Ali arrived. He owned the magnificent house and splendid garden. He had been watering some of the flower-beds further down in the garden. He was alarmed to see two boys at his tree. "What's going on?" he asked himself anxiously.

Imran and Uthman had absolutely no idea at all that Mr. Ali was standing right behind them watching. They had their backs turned to him. The two boys were totally engrossed in carrying out the plan they had hatched. Mr. Ali went on watching the two boys completely silently.

Uthman had learnt the great secret of plucking all fruit, but especially apples. That was to pluck only the fruit which comes easily away in the hand and not to pull hard on the apples. The apples which come softly and easily away are the ripest and the sweetest of them all. When he had plucked them Uthman then did something very silly. He dropped the apples behind him forgetting that they would bruise when they fell on the hard ground.

"Uthman, please don't throw the apples too far. They might end up in the swimming pool. I'm nearly dry now. I don't want to go in for another dip," said Imran, who was becoming tired and breathless from carrying Uthman.

"Don't worry, they won't be far behind us," replied Uthman, whose arms were becoming tired also from stretching to reach the best apples. They seemed to be just beyond his reach.

Neither boy had any idea at all that Mr. Ali had caught the apples. When Uthman had plucked four apples, he asked Imran, "Are four enough?"

"Yes, Yes," said Imran, "Don't pluck any more. We must hurry now before someone sees us." Uthman climbed clumsily down from Imran's shoulders.

Both of them turned around to look for the apples. Imagine their shock to see Mr. Ali standing right there with four apples in his hands! They were lost for words – Mr. Ali was their heADMASTER! Neither of them could say a word. Their throats were dry. They had swum like fish. Now they stood there with their mouths open like two fish.

"Well," said Mr. Ali, breaking the silence, "I think you'd both better get dressed and come over and talk with me."

Mr. Ali sat himself down on the bench which was beside the swimming pool. Both boys rushed over to their pile of clothes without uttering a single word. They dared not look at each other nor at Mr. Ali. If they had looked closely at him they might have seen that he seemed to be amused as he sat on the bench waiting for them. He was eating one of the sweet, sweet apples which Uthman had plucked. When they were dressed they approached him, feeling really terrified. They had been terribly worried that someone might see them and it had turned out much worse than they had imagined.

"So," began Mr. Ali, looking at both boys from above his glasses, "Did you have a good swim then?"

"Yes-s, w-we…" stuttered Imran, opening and closing his mouth more and more like a fish, "We were really hot so we thought that we should cool ourselves down a bit. We didn't know it was your house, did we Uthman?" Imran looked to Uthman for support, hoping that he might say something too. Uthman only looked silently from Imran to Mr. Ali and said nothing.

"I see," said Mr. Ali, looking a little stern, "You thought that nobody was watching you so why not have a good time?"

"Do you not know that you are always being watched by Allah?" said Mr. Ali, sitting the boys down, one on either side of him, "Allah sees you all the time. Whatever you are doing, whenever or wherever. Allah sees everything."

7

The boys had worried about an adult seeing them but they had never thought at all about Allah seeing them and seeing them all the time and everywhere! Here was something which needed thinking about.

"Sometimes I hide my crisps from Salwa my sister and eat them under the bedclothes. Does Allah see me eat my crisps?" asked Uthman. Really he was being a little cheeky and naughty with this question but Mr. Ali pretended not to notice.

"Of course! You must never think that you are not seen. Even though Salwa cannot see you eat your crisps, Allah sees you," said Mr. Ali.

"Sometimes," began Imran, "I hide my brother Faisal's colouring pens under my bed so that I can use them when he falls asleep. Does Allah know where I've hidden the pens and why I've hidden them?"

"Allah knows what we think. He knows all about us no matter where we are. Allah knows where everything is no matter where we hide it," replied Mr. Ali.

"So that means that when I play hide and seek with Salwa, Allah knows where we are hiding," said Uthman looking up at Mr. Ali.

The boys were awash with questions now.

"Can Allah see even if I hide in my wardrobe where it's really dark or when I turn off the bedroom light with the curtains closed?" asked Imran.

"Listen," began Mr. Ali seriously, "Allah sees the black ant on the black rock on a pitch black night with no moonlight and plenty of clouds. Allah sees everything everywhere no matter how dark it is. He sees everything all the time at the same time. When you, Uthman, hide your crisps from your sister Salwa and you, Imran, hide your pencils from your brother Faisal, Allah sees all of you at the same time and the ant on the black rock and everything that there is everywhere."

And Imran and Uthman sat quietly trying to understand how anyone could see absolutely everything at the same time. They couldn't even imagine it and so they were really amazed.

They were really interested now in what Mr. Ali was telling them. They wanted him to tell them more about Allah. Now they were studying together and they were close to each other in only the way people are who learn something together. Mr. Ali gave them an apple each, the same apples they had worked so hard to pluck from the tree. Then he began to tell them more about Allah.

"Allah has the power to do everything and anything. Allah says in the Qur'an that He is able to do all things. Allah made us, this world and the things in it like the flowers, the trees, the birds and the animals. He creates them all the time because you can see that there are baby creatures being born all the time. He made the moon, the sun, the sky and the stars. They all belong to Him. They all obey Allah's laws. The sun comes out and then it is daylight. The sun sets and then it becomes dark and then the moon and the stars appear. This is all Allah's doing."

The boys tried again really hard to imagine doing something so huge as changing the night and the day, and creating all the millions and millions of stars which were so far away in the sky, and they could not imagine it at all. It was too big.

"Does anyone help Allah to do all of this hard work?" asked Imran.

"No," said Mr. Ali, "As I've told you before. Allah has the power to do anything He wants, exactly whenever He wants."

"Allah is really great! Really marvellous! He does not need any help in all of this!" said Uthman. Lost in wonderment he gazed first at Mr. Ali and then Imran.

"Yes," said Mr. Ali, "Marvellous. Allah has no partners in all of this, no helpers. He does not need to sleep, eat or drink. So you can see that you should really worship One who does all of this. You can see how silly it would be to worship anyone else, or anything else." Mr. Ali poured them all a glass of the orange juice that had been standing on the table. They were surprised because they had not noticed it when they went swimming because they were too excited. They had not noticed it when they sat down with Mr. Ali because they were too scared.

"Does Allah have a mother or father?" Uthman puzzled aloud. He felt silly for asking the question almost as soon as it left his lips. But he need not have worried because Mr. Ali treated his question seriously. He was not angry with him.

"No," said Mr. Ali, shaking his head, "Allah has no mother or father, no brothers or sisters. If you think seriously you will see why that is impossible."

"Why is that?" both the boys asked at once.

"God is the One who has complete and total power over everything that is," Mr. Ali began, "If there were a brother, sister, mother, father, son or daughter of

God then they must also be gods."

"That's right," the boys both said at once and then laughed.

"So," Mr. Ali continued, "If there were all these different gods with control over everything they would have to fight over who had total control over everything."

"So of course there can only be One God who has control over everything," Uthman realised aloud.

"Allah is alone. A Muslim couldn't believe that there is any other god with Him," Mr. Ali continued, "A Muslim couldn't worship anything other than Allah because nothing is as marvellous as Him. And Allah is everlasting. He has always existed and He always will."

Imran could almost not imagine at all that Allah could be everlasting. So after thinking for a minute he asked another question altogether, "Why did Allah make us? Why did He make the world?"

"Allah made this world for us," said Mr. Ali, "Allah wants us to live a happy and peaceful life. He wants us to enjoy ourselves in this life. He wants us to live as Muslims as we have been taught in the Qur'an. If we live as Muslims, Allah is pleased with us and promises us paradise where He will reward us for our good actions."

"What do we need, to be Muslims?" asked Imran.

"Well," began Mr. Ali, "To be a Muslim we must always listen to our parents and treat them kindly. We must be helpful to everybody. We must never hurt anyone's feelings, nor be nasty to anyone. Allah doesn't like people who make fun of others, who tell lies or call people names."

"Does Allah get angry with people who do these things?" asked Uthman. He tried hard to imagine what the anger of the One who made the sun, the moon and the infinite stars could be like. He was rather frightened at the thought.

"Oh yes," answered Mr. Ali, "People who do these things make Allah angry. Allah tells us in the Qur'an that He loves the people who do things which He wants them to do, such as treating people well, looking after the poor, the orphans and the homeless. These things along with the prayer, the fast, the Zakah and the Hajj make people Muslims and then Allah loves them."

Now Imran tried to imagine what the love must be like, of the One who creates every living thing on the land, in the oceans and in the air. He just could not imagine how great it would be. But he knew that Allah's love and Allah's anger must be very great indeed.

"Please tell us more about what Allah likes and doesn't like, Mr. Ali," said Imran, looking at his headmaster in excitement.

"Allah wants us to look after old people and help them, like our parents when they become old. He doesn't like us to take things which do not belong to us without asking. He hates us to use bad language," he said.

"Uthman and I never use bad language, do we Uthman?" interrupted Imran.

"I'm pleased to hear it Imran," said Mr. Ali.

"Is Allah angry with people who do things thinking that Allah doesn't see them?" asked Imran who suddenly remembered just why he and Uthman were sitting with Mr. Ali. He had become really worried because of what he and Uthman had done in Mr. Ali's garden.

"Well yes," replied Mr. Ali, "But the two of you didn't really know that you were doing something which Allah dislikes. I think Allah will forgive you, because I have forgiven you and Allah is more forgiving than me, Allah is the Most Forgiving of all." He added, "Allah is the friend of the believers." Mr. Ali smiled at the two.

"Is Allah really the friend of the believers?" cried Imran in excitement, nearly knocking Mr. Ali's glass of orange out of his hand.

"I want to be the friend of Allah, Mr. Ali. If I am a Muslim, will Allah be my friend?" asked Uthman,

"Yes, Allah tells us in the Qur'an that He is the friend of the believers," replied Mr. Ali, as he finished his last sip of orange.

Imran had thought of something new. "Can we talk to Allah?" he asked.

"Yes, of course," Mr. Ali said, "We DO talk to Allah every time we pray to Him. Just as He always sees us, He always hears us and listens to us. He listens to our prayers when we talk to Him."

"But which language does Allah understand? We can only speak English and Arabic," asked Imran, looking at Uthman who had been thinking the same question but had started to let Imran ask all the questions in case he asked something stupid.

Mr. Ali looked at both boys and smiled at them, saying, "But Allah created everything including all the languages. Of course He knows and understands everything, every language. He understands you whether you speak German, French, Urdu, Chinese or Dutch. He knows them all." He said all this to put the boys at their ease.

When they understood this they realised that they could freely and easily talk in prayer to Allah any time they wanted to. They both realised that the first thing they wanted was to ask Him to forgive them for coming into Mr. Ali's garden without permission.

After Mr. Ali had finished telling the boys about Allah, they both apologised to him for coming into his garden and plucking his apples without permission.

But Mr. Ali said, "I've been so pleased for your visit. I'd be very happy if you would come to visit me again very often."

The boys told him that they would go home to ask Allah to forgive them for what they had done.

"I'm sure Allah will forgive you," said Mr. Ali, "You didn't really know that you were doing something wrong. Allah forgives those who promise never to do what they did wrong again." He patted them on their heads and they left him to go home.

On their way home, Imran and Uthman worked together on composing a little poem about Allah. It went like this:

ALLAH IS GREAT, ALLAH IS GREAT,
HE IS THE GREATEST OF ALL THE GREAT,
HE IS THE KING OF ALL THE KINGS,
AND THE LORD OF ALL THE THINGS,
HE MADE THIS WORLD, ALONE,
WE BELONG TO HIM ALONE.
TO HIM WE TURN WITH ALL OUR NEEDS,
WE KNOW ALLAH LOVES US
AND WE LOVE HIM.

QUESTIONS
FOR YOU TO ANSWER

1) What did Imran and Uthman do in Mr Ali's garden?

2) Do you think they did the right thing to go into his garden? Why?

3) What do you think was the most important thing which Mr Ali told the boys?

4) Name five things which Mr Ali told the boys about Allah.

5) How can be friends of Allah?

6) What makes Allah angry?

7) What pleases Allah?

8) What should a Muslim not do? Why?

9) What should a Muslim do? Why?

10) Did you do anything to please Allah today?

11) Write something you know about Allah and then show it to your teacher or mother or father.